BITCOINS & TULIP MANIA
A Beginners' Guide
to Cryptocurrency Profits

Brian Wilkes

฿฿฿฿฿฿฿฿฿฿

BITCOINS
&
TULIP MANIA

A Beginners' Guide
to Cryptocurrency Profits

by Brian Wilkes

author of

"HYPERINFLATION: How To Prepare For The Coming Dollar Collapse"

฿฿฿฿฿฿฿฿฿฿

Table of Contents

DISCLAIMER: Brian Wilkes ("Author") provides this book as-is for informational purposes only.
NO INVESTMENT ADVICE: The Content is for informational purposes only, you should not construe any such information or other material as legal, tax, investment, financial, or other advice. Nothing contained in this book constitutes a solicitation, recommendation, endorsement, or offer by the Author any third party service provider to buy or sell any securities or other financial instruments in this or in in any other jurisdiction in which such solicitation or offer would be unlawful under the securities laws of such jurisdiction. All Content in this book is information of a general nature and does not address the circumstances of any particular individual or entity. Nothing in the Content constitutes professional and/or financial advice, nor does any information in this book constitutes a comprehensive or complete statement of the matters discussed or the law relating thereto. The Author is not a fiduciary by virtue of any person's use of or access to the Content. You alone assume the sole responsibility of evaluating the merits and risks associated with the use of any information or other Content before making any decisions based on such information or other Content. In exchange for using the book, you agree not to hold the Author, the publisher, or any third party service provider liable for any possible claim for damages arising from any decision you make based on information or other Content made available to you.
INVESTMENT RISKS: There are risks associated with investing in currencies and securities. Investing in stocks, bonds, exchange traded funds, mutual funds, cryptocurrencies, precious metals, and money market funds involve risk of loss. Loss of principal is possible. Some high risk investments may use leverage, which will accentuate gains and losses. Foreign investing involves special risks, including a greater volatility and political, economic and currency risks and differences in accounting methods. A security's or a firm's past investment performance is not a guarantee or predictor of future investment performance.
THIRD PARTY LINKED SITES: As a convenience to you, the Author may provide hyperlinks to web sites operated by third parties. Because the Author has no control over such sites or their content, the Author is not responsible for the availability of such external sites or their content, and the Author does not adopt, endorse, nor is responsible or liable for any such sites or content, including advertising, products or other materials, on or available through such sites or resources. Other web sites may provide links to the Site or Content. The Author does not endorse such sites and shall not be responsible or liable for any links from those sites to the Book or Content, or for any content, advertising, products or other materials available on or through such other sites, or any loss or damages incurred in connection therewith.

About The Author

Brian Wilkes is a retired award-winning network journalist. He admits that for years he delivered stock market reports on the air without truly comprehending what he was saying. He then realized that few of his colleagues did, either! Since then, he has learned.

At this writing, he resides in southern Illinois.

Introduction

Bitcoin has been going strong for 10 years, and its popularity has soared. This digital currency reached a value of $19,260 in December 2017, and some analysts think it can break the $1-million mark by the end of 2025. Some think that's conservative, and it could break five million dollars by that date. In order to make the best returns on Bitcoin investments, you need to understand what it really is and how it works.

You also need to know the best way to obtain Bitcoins and the best strategies to increase the value of your investment. This guide will show you all of this and more. Many people still think that Bitcoin is a scam, but it certainly is not. However, there have been some scams in the cryptocurrency world, and in this guide we will show you how to avoid these and stay safe.

We have worked hard to ensure that everything in this guide is up to date and explained in the simplest ways. Bitcoin and the underlying blockchain technology are fairly complex but you will be able to easily comprehend these by reading this guide.

Bitcoin started out with a value of zero and has hit highs of almost $20,000 as of this writing in June 2020. It is a valuable commodity. Once you have your Bitcoins, learn how to keep them safe.

Although Bitcoin is a volatile commodity, it should be possible for you to make a good return on your investment if you follow the advice in this guide. While there are no guarantees with any form of investing, the advice provided here has worked well for others in the past, including this author. But before we get into the details of crypto, let's look at another investment with wildly rising values

This book is divided into three sections: **History and Theory**, **Plan A**, and **Plan B**.

SECTION I: History and Theory

Tulip Mania

Tulip mania was a period in the Dutch Golden Age during which contract prices for some bulbs of the recently introduced and fashionable tulip reached extraordinarily high levels and then dramatically collapsed in February 1637. It is generally considered the first recorded speculative bubble. The term "tulip mania" is now often used metaphorically to refer to any large economic bubble when asset prices deviate from intrinsic values.

In Europe, formal **futures markets** appeared in the Dutch Republic during the 17th century. At the peak of tulip mania, in February 1637, some single tulip bulbs sold for more than 10 times the annual income of a skilled craftsman. The high asset prices may also have been driven by expectations of a parliamentary decree that contracts could be voided for a small cost, thus lowering the risk to buyers.

Tulip mania went largely unnoticed at the time, but two centuries later it was used as a bad example for irrational investment. The 1637 event was popularized in 1841 by the book ***Extraordinary Popular Delusions and the Madness of Crowds,*** written by Charles Mackay. At one point 12 acres or 5 hectares of land were offered for a single *Semper Augustus* bulb. Many modern scholars feel that the mania was not as extraordinary as Mackay described, and argue that not enough price data is available to prove that a tulip-bulb bubble actually occurred.

The tulip was different from every other flower known to Northern Europe at that time, with a saturated intense petal color that no other plant had, especially in colder climates. The appearance of the tulip as a status symbol at this time coincides with the rise of newly independent Holland's trade fortunes. No longer the Spanish Netherlands, its economic resources could now be channeled into commerce and the country embarked on its Golden Age. Amsterdam merchants were at the center of the lucrative East Indies trade, where one voyage could yield profits of 400%.

In the Northern Hemisphere, tulips bloom in April and May for about one week. During the plant's dormant phase from June to September, bulbs can be uprooted and moved about, so actual purchases in the **spot market** occurred during these months. During the rest of the year, florists, or tulip traders, signed contracts before a notary to buy tulips at the end of the season – effectively, **futures contracts**. Thus the Dutch, who developed many of the techniques of modern finance, created a market for tulip bulbs. **Short selling** was banned by an edict of 1610, which was reiterated or strengthened in 1621 and 1630, and again in 1636. Short sellers were not prosecuted under these edicts, but futures contracts were deemed unenforceable, so traders could repudiate deals if faced with a loss. The tulip market collapsed abruptly in February, 1636.

As the flowers grew in popularity, professional growers paid higher and higher prices for bulbs with a virus that created multicolored, spotted, and striped blossoms, and prices rose steadily. In 1636 the Dutch created a type of formal futures market where contracts to buy bulbs at the end of the season were bought and sold. Traders met in "colleges" at taverns and buyers were required to pay a 2.5% "wine money" fee, up to a maximum of three guilders per trade. Neither party paid an initial **margin**, nor a mark-to-market margin, and all contracts were with the individual counter-parties rather than with the Exchange. The Dutch described tulip contract trading as *windhandel* ("wind trade"), because no bulbs were actually changing hands. The modern equivalent might be *vaporware.* The entire business was accomplished on the margins of Dutch economic life, usually taverns, not in the Exchange itself.

By 1636, the tulip bulb became the fourth leading export product of the Netherlands, after gin, herrings, and cheese. The price of tulips skyrocketed because of speculation in tulip futures among people who never saw the bulbs.

Tulip mania reached its peak during the winter of 1636–37, when some bulbs were reportedly changing hands ten times in a day. No deliveries were ever made to fulfil any of these contracts, because in February 1637, tulip bulb contract prices collapsed abruptly and the trade of tulips ground to a halt. The collapse began in Haarlem, when, for the first time, buyers apparently refused to show up at a routine bulb auction. This may have been because Haarlem was then suffering from an outbreak of bubonic plague. The plague may have helped to create a culture of fatalistic risk-taking that allowed the speculation to skyrocket in the first place; this outbreak might also have helped to burst the bubble. The plague and its aftermath may have also created a demand for items of color and beauty in the lives of those who could afford it.

Group of goods allegedly exchanged for a single bulb of the *Viceroy* strain:

Two lasts (a "last" is about 2 tons) of wheat, 448ƒ;
Four lasts of rye, 558ƒ;
Four fat oxen, 480ƒ;
Eight fat swine, 240ƒ;
Twelve fat sheep, 120ƒ;
Two hogsheads (a "hoghead" is 58-63 US gallons) of wine, 70ƒ;
Four tuns (a "tun" is about 250 gallons) of beer, 32ƒ;
Two tuns of butter, 192ƒ;
1,000 lbs. of cheese, 120ƒ;
A complete bed, 100ƒ;
A suit of clothes, 80ƒ;
<u>A silver drinking cup, 60ƒ;</u>
Total: 2500ƒ

*Note: 1 florin in 1635 had the buying power of **fl. 28.42** today (€ 12.90, $14.42), making this collection worth over €63,150 / $71,000 in 2020*

Mackay's account was largely sourced from a 1797 work by Johann Beckmann titled **A History of Inventions, Discoveries, and Origins.** Beckmann's account was primarily sourced to three anonymous pamphlets published in 1637 with an agenda against financial speculation.

By 1636, tulips were traded on the exchanges of numerous Dutch towns and cities. This encouraged trading in tulips by all members of society; Mackay recounted people selling or trading their other possessions in order to speculate in the tulip market, such as an offer of 12 acres (49,000 sq. m.) of land for one of two existing *Semper Augustus* bulbs, or a single bulb of the *Viceroy* that, Mackay claimed, was purchased in exchange for a basket of goods (shown in table) worth 2,500 florins.

Many individuals grew suddenly rich. Everyone imagined that the passion for tulips would last forever, and that the wealthy from every part of the world would send to Holland, and pay whatever prices were asked for them. Everyone from rich merchants down to house servants dabbled in tulips, according to Mackay. Later historians believe the trading was limited to wealthy merchants and craftspeople, with the nobility and working class largely absent.

People were purchasing bulbs at higher and higher prices, intending to re-sell them for a profit. Such a scheme could not last unless someone was ultimately willing to pay such high prices and take possession of the bulbs. In February 1637, tulip traders could no longer find new buyers willing to pay increasingly inflated prices for their bulbs. As this realization set in, the demand for tulips collapsed, and prices plummeted. The speculative bubble burst. Some were left holding contracts to purchase tulips at prices now ten times greater than those on the open market, while others found themselves in possession of bulbs now worth a fraction of the price they had paid.

In Mackay's account, the panicked tulip speculators sought help from the Dutch government, which responded by declaring that anyone who had bought contracts to purchase bulbs in the future could void their contract by payment of a 10 percent fee. Attempts were made to resolve the situation to the satisfaction of all parties, but these were unsuccessful. The mania finally ended, Mackay says, with individuals stuck with the bulbs they held at the end of the crash. No court would enforce payment of a contract, since judges regarded the debts as contracted through gambling, and thus not enforceable by law.

Although prices had risen, money had not changed hands between buyers and sellers. Profits were never realized for sellers; unless sellers had made other purchases on credit in expectation of the profits, the collapse in prices did not cause anyone to lose money.

Fashions Change

At the beginning of the 19th century the hyacinth replaced the tulip as the fashionable flower. When hyacinths were introduced, florists strove with one another to grow beautiful hyacinth flowers, as demand was strong. As people became more accustomed to hyacinths, their prices began to fall as the tulip prices had.

On February 24, 1637, the self-regulating guild of Dutch florists, in a decision that was later ratified by the Dutch Parliament, announced that all futures contracts written after November 30, 1636, and before the re-opening of the cash market in the early Spring, were to be interpreted as option contracts. They did this by simply relieving the futures buyers of the obligation to buy the future tulips, forcing them merely to compensate the sellers with a small fixed percentage of the contract price. Before this parliamentary decree, the purchaser of a tulip contract — known in modern finance as a forward contract — was legally obliged to buy the bulbs. The decree changed the nature of these contracts, so that if the current market price fell, the purchaser could opt to pay a penalty and forgo receipt of the bulb, rather than pay the full contracted price. This change in law meant that, in modern terminology, the futures contracts had been transformed into options contracts, which were extremely favorable to the buyers.

Many of the sources telling of the woes of tulip mania, such as the anti-speculative pamphlets that were later reported by Beckmann and Mackay, have been cited as evidence of the extent of the economic damage. These pamphlets were not written by victims of a bubble, but were primarily religiously motivated. The upheaval was viewed as a perversion of the moral order—proof that "concentration on the earthly, rather than the heavenly flower could have dire consequences". Thus, it is possible that a relatively minor economic event took on a life of its own as a morality tale.

In November 2013, Nout Wellink, former president of the Dutch Central Bank, described Bitcoin as "worse than the tulip mania," adding, "At least then you got a tulip, now you get nothing." We're about to show you how to avoid that trap.

What IS Money?

You have probably heard of Bitcoin but you may not be completely sure what it is. okay, because by the time you have read through this guide you will know what it is and how you can make money with it. Bitcoin is a **cryptocurrency** which is another term that you need to be familiar with. The other important thing that we will explain is the technology behind Bitcoin and most other cryptocurrencies, **blockchain.**

Before we get into the details of Bitcoin, it is important that you understand what cryptocurrencies are and how they work. Even more basically, what is money?

Medium of Exchange

Money gradually replaced barter so that buyer and seller could better calculate relative value.

In barter, if I had a rabbit you wanted and you had a basket of berries I wanted, we would exchange, and each walked away thinking they had received equal value. This became more complicated with larger deals, and eventually people translated the perceived value of each item into a common medium of exchange: drachma, talents, dollars. Coins were struck in metals that had agreed-upon intrinsic value – gold, silver, copper, and copper allows such as bronze and cupronickel. Financial guru Robert Kiyosaki calls these "God's money".

These became heavy in larger quantities, and so the "note" or paper currency was introduced. This was an IOU promising redemption in precious metals at some future date. Soon, that convertibility would end worldwide.

Fiat Currency and Cryptocurrency.

Those dollars, pounds, and euros in your wallet today are known as **fiat currency.** The term fiat currency comes from Latin for "let it be done", and refers to anything that has value only because it has been declared so by the government or another ruling authority. It has as much real value as an IOU scrawled on a Post-It note, and is solely dependent on the public's good faith in the government that issued it.

Until 1968, the "silver certificate" was convertible to silver coins or granules. The wording on the bills specified "*X* dollars in silver coin payable to the bearer on demand". This meant that the Treasury was required to keep in its vaults enough silver dollars to cover all of the silver certificates in circulation. On June 4, 1963, the Silver Purchase Act was repealed, and the issuing of silver certificates ended. On June 28, 1968, redemption of silver certificates for silver ended. I still remember people lining up at the banks, exiting with moneybags of coins and bullion.

Until 1971, the US dollar was backed by gold, with the value of the dollar pegged at $1/35^{th}$ of a troy ounce of gold. Foreign governments redeemed their crates of dollars for US gold bullion. President Richard Nixon took the country off the gold standard because the country had effectively gone bankrupt fighting the war in Vietnam and the "war on poverty" at the same time. This led to a lack of faith in now-devalued the US dollar, and oil producing countries demanded payment in gold bullion. You may remember the 1974 Oil Embargo, resulting from the Organization of Petroleum Exporting Countries (OPEC) deciding they would no longer accept devalued dollars, and demanded payment in gold instead. As a result, the price of a barrel of crude dropped when paid in gold but rose when paid in US dollars. We remember the culture shock when the price of gasoline first broke $1 a gallon at the pump.

Who manages it?
Fiat: The government that issues it.
Crypto: A network of computers running open source code

How does it hold its value?
Fiat: Confidence in the government that issues it
Crypto: Primarily based on supply and demand

How is it secured?
Fiat: By select third parties like banks and governments.
Crypto: By a network of computers that verify every transaction.

Can I buy things with it?
Fiat: Yes, but typically only in the country that issues it
Crypto: Yes, but only where merchants accept it

Cryptocurrencies were invented by accident. The inventor of Bitcoin, Satoshi Nakamoto (possibly a pseudonym), created a peer-to-peer electronic cash system, and Bitcoin was a byproduct of this system. Before this, there had been numerous attempts to create a digital cash system, but all had failed.

The key to the success of Nakamoto's system was that it provided a **decentralized financial network** rather than the established centralized system. If you wanted to set up your own digital cash system you would need to create a payment network that provided three key things:

1. Accounts
2. Balances
3. Transactions

Why A Global Digital Currency?

The financial crisis of 2007–2008, also known as the Global Financial Crisis (GFC), was a severe worldwide financial event. Excessive risk-taking by banks combined with a downturn in the subprime lending market in the United States culminated with the bankruptcy of Lehman Brothers on September 15, 2008 and an international banking crisis. The crisis sparked the **Great Recession,** a global recession, which, until the coronavirus recession, was the most severe recession since the **Great Depression**. It was also followed by the European debt crisis, which began with a deficit in Greece in late 2009, and the 2008–2011 Icelandic financial crisis.

It is important to remember that the Great Depression of 1929 did not affect the world equally. In Canada, which has tighter banking regulations, it was almost unfelt. Much of Latin America experienced economic growth during that period. However the world's economies had become more tightly intertwined since then, with all nations abandoning gold-backed currencies for fiat currencies, floated on world markets against each other. This time, the whole world felt it.

Governments were forced to provide then-unprecedented bailouts and stimulus in 2008 to avoid a further collapse, encourage lending, restore faith in the integral commercial paper markets, and provide banks with enough funds to allow customers to make withdrawals. The values of major currencies fluctuated wildly, and the runaway inflation devoured the value of savings and retirement funds. By the time it was over, it cost $29-trillion in federal bailouts in the US alone.

From the beginning of the GFC in 2007 to this writing in 2020, we have seen a cumulative rate of inflation of 23.7%.

If you had put $100 of cash in a cookie jar in 2009, you would have lost almost $20 of buying power by 2020.

Techies developed cryptocurrencies in the wake of the GFC to provide an inflation-resistant global alternative to fiat currency. If you had bought $100 of Bitcoin when it first became available in January 2009, you would have $3,629,600 today.

What are Cryptocurrencies?

Cryptocurrency is a medium for exchange online. A cryptocurrency has a number of cryptographical functions which are there to support financial transactions. Most cryptocurrencies use the **blockchain** technology platform (more on this a little later) as it offers immutability, transparency and decentralization.

Cryptocurrencies are digital cash for the digital age. It's similar to regular money, but it's digital-only, so there are no bills or coins to carry around.

Cryptocurrencies are not controlled by any central powers – not yet at least. This is deliberate because the whole idea of cryptocurrency and Bitcoin is that they provide immunity from government interference and control.

A cryptocurrency can be transferred from one person to another by using **public and private keys.** There are comparatively minimal processing fees involved with cryptocurrency transactions, which are part of their appeal. Usually financial institutions have high charges for any monetary transaction.

What is Bitcoin?

Bitcoin is a cryptocurrency first introduced on October 31, 2008 in a computer science paper that described how it would work. A few months later, on January 3, 2009, the code was released and the first Bitcoins appeared.

Bitcoin is often compared to gold in that there is a limited supply. The maximum number of bitcoins that will ever enter circulation is fixed at 21 million. Unlike gold, however, bitcoin is digital, making it far easier to divide, transfer, and store.

Bitcoin is the oldest and most well-known cryptocurrency, but there are hundreds of others. Some cryptocurrencies, like **Litecoin** and **Bitcoin Cash**, share Bitcoin's core characteristics but explore new ways to process transactions. Others offer a wider range of features. **Ethereum,** for example, can be used to run applications and create contracts.

A problem that all payment networks face is "double spending". This is all about preventing spending the same amount twice. Up until the creation of Nakamoto's system this had always been achieved using central server balance records (this is still in existence today).

With a decentralized payment network there is no central server. Instead, every single network entity or node has to perform its job properly. They all need to have a list of transactions so they can monitor if future transactions are a "double spend" or valid.

All of the peers of a decentralized payment network have to agree on everything. There must be complete consensus. If this doesn't happen then the transaction will not take place. The problem was how to achieve this total consensus without a central server. Nakamoto figured this out.

The Transactional Properties of Cryptocurrencies

In order for a cryptocurrency system to work effectively there must be a number of properties in place:

Immutability: After a cryptocurrency transaction is confirmed, it cannot be changed. Nobody in the world can change a cryptocurrency transaction, not even presidents or monarchs. It is an immutable record.

If you send crypto to someone else, that's it. There is no turning back. If you make a mistake or get scammed, you are stuck with the situation. You do not have the opportunity to reverse the transaction, as you might with a bank debit card or a credit card purchase.

Pseudonymous: Cryptocurrency accounts and transactions have no connection to real world identities. You will receive a Bitcoin on an address which is a randomly seeming chain of about 30 characters. You can analyze the transaction flow, but you can't usually connect the transaction to a real person through the address.

Transaction Speed: It doesn't take long to propagate transactions and confirm them. Usually this all takes place in minutes. The network for cryptocurrency transactions is global, so it doesn't matter where the transaction originates and terminates.

High Security: The highest levels of transaction security are essential for a cryptocurrency network with all funds locked in a public key cryptography system. Only someone that has a private key can send cryptocurrency. This makes the system extremely secure.

No Permissions: A cryptocurrency system is a "permissionless" system. You do not require the permission of anyone or any authority to make a cryptocurrency transaction. There is no gatekeeper with a cryptocurrency system.

The Monetary Properties of Cryptocurrency

Now you know the transaction properties of cryptocurrency you need to understand the monetary properties. These are:

Controlled, Limited Supply: Most cryptocurrencies have a limit on the number of tokens supplied. Taking Bitcoin as an example there will be a decrease of supply over time and experts estimate that the final number of Bitcoin tokens will happen around 2140. Experts say that only 21 million Bitcoins will be the limit.

To control the supply of cryptocurrency tokens, a schedule is written in the underlying code. Using this code you, can approximately calculate today the monetary supply of a cryptocurrency for any given future date.

Not Debt: With conventional or "fiat" money underwritten by a government, the bank account you hold is created by debt. All of the entries in your account are debts. It is really an IOU system. A cryptocurrency is not a debt.

The launch of cryptocurrencies has been controversial because they are a direct attack on or circumvention of the monetary policy of most nations. Governments or central banks cannot change cryptocurrencies. Therefore, these are immune to inflation and deflation caused by the manipulation of the monetary supply by governments and central banks.

Bitcoin is a cryptocurrency and a virtual type of money. It's really like having an online version of money or cash. You can use Bitcoin to purchase products and services as more and more vendors are accepting Bitcoin as a form of payment these days. Some countries feel very threatened by Bitcoin and have banned it completely.

There are no physical Bitcoin tokens. You may have seen pictures of Bitcoins, but these are fabrications, artistic presentations of what a Bitcoin might look like if it was minted like a silver or gold coin. The true worth of a Bitcoin resides in the private codes they have imprinted inside them.

Every Bitcoin is just a computer file stored in what's called a **digital wallet.** We will discuss digital wallets in more detail in a later chapter. If you have a digital wallet, then other people can send you Bitcoins or fractions of them. You can also send Bitcoins or fractions to others using your digital wallet.

Every Bitcoin transaction is recorded publicly using blockchain technology. This is a transparent network where anyone can trace the history of Bitcoin transactions. All records in the blockchain are immutable, meaning that you cannot copy transactions, change the amount of Bitcoins owned, or use Bitcoins that you don't own.

There are several ways that you can purchase Bitcoins including:

- You can purchase them using your native domestic currency through a cryptocurrency exchange
- You can sell products and services in exchange for Bitcoins
- You can use a Bitcoin ATM
- You can "mine" Bitcoins

The practice of mining Bitcoins has been going on for a while. In order to do this you will need high end computer equipment and lots of it. These computers perform complex algorithms to guess secret codes. If your computers guess right, you get Bitcoins as a reward.

We will not be recommending mining as a way of obtaining Bitcoins in this guide. There are only a limited number of Bitcoins so the process of mining is now incredibly complex. You could spend years mining for Bitcoin and spend a great deal of money on computer equipment and software without earning any Bitcoins.

You may be wondering why Bitcoins are so valuable. When Bitcoin first started it had no value but in five years a single Bitcoin was worth around $1,000. At the time of writing a Bitcoin is worth around $8,000.

Why this jump? Well there are a number of other things in life that have value. Diamonds and gold are a good example. Bitcoins have value because people are willing to trade them for real products and services and also buy them for cash.

People like the idea that no governments or central banks control Bitcoins. They also like the fact that Bitcoin transactions are pretty anonymous. Yes, there is a record of all Bitcoin transactions but very few include real world identities.

Bitcoin transactions are also irreversible. If you accept payment via credit cards or PayPal for example, you can suddenly find a buyer has demanded a refund from the carrier. You as the vendor seldom have recourse. By comparison, a cryptocurrency transaction is not reversible because there is not a central authority to which either party can appeal. *Caveat emptor, caveat vendor* – let both buyer and seller beware.

Summation: Cryptocurrency is outside the system. It doesn't depend on the Federal Reserve Bank, or the Treasury, or Wall Street to set its value. It depends instead on the demand millions of investors around the world – the free market.

To quote Robert Kiyosaki, gold and silver with their intrinsic value are "God's money", fiat currencies with values set by governments and their central banks are "government's money", and cryptocurrency is "the people's money".

SECTION II: PLAN A

Bitcoin Investing

One of your first decision is why you want Bitcoin (NOTE: from this point, we'll use "Bitcoin" as a generic word for cryptocurrency unless otherwise specified.) Do you want to use Bitcoin as a global medium of exchange, to buy and sell products and services? Is anonymity important to you? Do you want to transfer part of your wealth beyond the reach of governments and banks? Or, do you simply want to invest as a hedge against inflation, or to speculate on the rising value of Bitcoin? Those answers will help you determine the best of several paths and services.

The first thing that you need to know is that Bitcoin is volatile. The value of a single Bitcoin has gone up and down over the years. This is not particularly a bad thing as other investments go up and down too. You need to be a smart investor with Bitcoin.

Why Does Bitcoin Experience Value Jumps?

So many people are reliant on the Internet these days. People get very frustrated if they are out and about and cannot find a WiFi connection to use the Internet with their mobile devices. Whether this is a good or bad thing is of no consequence when it comes to Bitcoin investing. The important thing is that growing use of the Internet is good for Bitcoin.

Over the years since the launch of Bitcoin it has attracted investors from all corners of the world. Being a true global digital currency that is available to all (in theory) it is no surprise that it has generated a lot of excitement.

Another good reason why the value of Bitcoin has risen so rapidly is because it is a scarce resource that is actually useful. Most people know that there is only so much gold that we can mine. Each year there is less and less gold left in the Earth. Therefore it has great value.

You can apply the same logic to Bitcoin. There will only ever be **21 million Bitcoin.** As time passes this number will dwindle and the value increases. It is now very hard to mine Bitcoin and this is only going to get tougher.

Investors really like the fact that Bitcoin represents predictable and sound monetary policy that all can verify. At any time you can see how many Bitcoins are in circulation and how many new ones have been created.

You can easily trade Bitcoin for some products and services. If you have a gold investment then this is not a liquid asset. You would have to sell some of your gold stock for cash before you could purchase anything.

It is very easy to make cross border transactions using Bitcoin. There are no governments or banks involved. You can send Bitcoin securely in minutes to anywhere in the world. Transaction fees are very low compared to fiat currency transactions.

We have the Internet to thank for the rise in popularity and value of Bitcoin. The Internet has made the sharing of information easy wherever you are and this concept will underpin the success of Bitcoin as a global and verifiable currency.

The Price of Bitcoin

You will not find an official price for Bitcoin anywhere. It is not the same as fiat currencies. It is all about how much someone is willing to pay for a Bitcoin or fraction of a Bitcoin. A good reference for this price is the Bitcoin Price Index provided by Coin Desk which you can find at www.coindesk.com/price/bitcoin .

You will usually see the price as the estimate of the value of one Bitcoin. Most cryptocurrency exchanges will let you buy as many Bitcoins as you want and even offer fractions of Bitcoins for sale.

When should you buy Bitcoins?

There are no guarantees with any investments. The history of Bitcoin shows that it tends to increase in value really fast and then slow down and fall until it is stable. This is a cycle that you need to learn and understand.

There are some great tools available that you can use to analyze the price history of Bitcoin. Probably the best two are:

1. **Cryptowatch**   https://cryptowat.ch/
2. **Bitcoin Wisdom** https://bitcoinwisdom.com/

One thing about Bitcoin that is really attractive to investors is that it is never affected by the financial stability of a country. So if there is speculation that a major currency will fall, such as the UK Pound with all of the Brexit issues, then if the currency devalues this will have an impact on other world currencies.

So you need to think globally with Bitcoin. Don't just look at what is happening in the United States, or Europe or China. How is the economy of the world changing?

Go For Long Term Bitcoin Investment

You may have read that there are people making excellent short term gains trading Bitcoin. While this may be true you need expert knowledge and it is a risky strategy. We strongly recommend that you go for a long term Bitcoin investment strategy.

Here is why. If you invested $1000 in Bitcoin in October 2017, two years later in October 2019 you would have made a profit of more than $700, providing you with a return on investment of over 70%. That is a staggering return.

Despite these kinds of returns being possible you should still treat Bitcoin as a risky asset to invest in. If you are not prepared to make high risk investments then maybe Bitcoin is not for you. You have seen an example of the kind of rewards that are possible so you need to decide if it is right for you.

Bitcoin Investment Strategies

There are different ways that you can invest in Bitcoin. We will look at the most popular ways here:

Long Term Buy-and-Hold

This is the Bitcoin investment strategy that we recommend. Here you will buy Bitcoin at a certain price and hold on to it for a period of time in the hope that the value will increase. You may also see this strategy called "holding".

When you decide to buy-and-hold it is very important that you do not just take anyone's advice on whether Bitcoin will rise or fall. You need to know how Bitcoin works and do your homework using the tools available to come to a decision yourself.

If you are going to adopt a buy-and-hold Bitcoin investment strategy then we suggest that you do the following:

1. Do not invest more than you can comfortably afford to lose. As we said earlier, Bitcoin is a high risk investment and this should be in your thoughts at all times.

2. When you have purchased Bitcoins, don't leave them in an exchange wallet. Get your own wallet and move them there. We will discuss the different types if cryptocurrency wallet and their advantages and disadvantages in a later chapter.
3. Use a reputable exchange to make your Bitcoin purchases. This may cost you a bit more but it is better to be safe than sorry.
4. Don't purchase all of your Bitcoins in just one trade. Use the principle of Dollar cost averaging (DCA) and commit to purchasing a certain amount every month (or more frequently) throughout the course of the year. When you do this you pay average prices during the year.

Short Term Bitcoin Trading

This is when you buy Bitcoins at a low price and then sell them at a higher price to realize a profit. The time frame for these investments is short, usually up to three months. We do not recommend that you start out with short term Bitcoin trading.

As you learn more about Bitcoin and observe trends, you can consider moving to a shorter term trading strategy. It is certainly possible and there are some very large players in the Bitcoin market making profits regularly on short term Bitcoin trades. You need to learn how to trade properly to make this work which takes time and practice.

Mining for Bitcoins

In order to make any kind of profit with Bitcoin mining, you need to invest in a lot of high end computer equipment and get the cheapest electricity that you can find. And even then, there are no guarantees!

Mining has become a lot harder over the years. There are fewer and fewer Bitcoins to find and more and more people mining. It is just not a cost effective way to invest in Bitcoin in our opinion. Use the money you would spend on equipment and electricity to buy and hold Bitcoin instead.

You may have heard of **cloud mining** for Bitcoin. The idea here is that you pay for a service that will mine on your behalf using the web. In our experience, these are either scams or so expensive an investment that you might as well just use the money to purchase your Bitcoins.

Doubling Your Bitcoins

Have you seen websites that claim that they can double your Bitcoin holdings? Or maybe you have come across sites that claim they will pay you high levels of interest every day on your Bitcoins? We have one word for these kinds of websites:

SCAMS!

There are lots of websites that offer high yield investment programs (HYIP) and almost all of these are scams too. What happens here is that these sites take money from people all round the Internet in exchange for high returns. They use the money that they get from new people signing up to pay high returns to the initial investors which creates a buzz.

Then, a few months later, the website simply disappears! Most people lose their money and they have no way to get it back. Don't fall for these Ponzi scheme type scams. You cannot double the amount of Bitcoins that you have using these sites. It is more likely that you will lose all of your Bitcoins.

How Bitcoin Really Works

To be profitable with Bitcoin, you have to know how it really works. We will explain everything that is involved including the underlying technology, which is blockchain. We are not going to go into a lot of technical detail about blockchain, so don't worry. But you do need to understand the principles of it.

You connect to the blockchain community using a computer network. This network has Bitcoin ledgers using blockchain. All Bitcoin transactions are compiled into blocks, and then these blocks connect in a chain-like formation. This is where the name blockchain comes from.

The Bitcoin Process

If you want to make a Bitcoin transaction, you will use your wallet to send out a request to all of the nodes (computers) on the entire Bitcoin network. The nodes use special algorithms (a set of rules and calculations) which validate the Bitcoin transaction.

Your Bitcoin transaction has to be verified and confirmed and after this it is combined with some other transactions to make a new data block and eventually a blockchain. All new blocks are added to the end of the blockchain. At this stage the transaction is final and immutable.

It usually takes between 10 minutes and 45 minutes to process a Bitcoin transaction. A Bitcoin transaction never happens immediately. There can be no changes to the transaction once it is finalized. The receiver of your Bitcoin transaction then sees this in their wallet.

Bitcoin Miners are Essential

We have mentioned Bitcoin miners several times in this guide, because these people are very important. Why? Because they are the keepers of the Bitcoin ledgers. If you think of a gold miner working tirelessly to find gold, Bitcoin miners are doing the same thing trying to find increasingly scarce Bitcoins.

The Bitcoin miners verify and confirm all Bitcoin transactions. They really are the lifeblood of the Bitcoin system. Without them, the whole thing would not work. There would be no new blocks created for the blockchain. This is why they are rewarded occasionally with valuable Bitcoins.

If blocks are not added to the blockchain, then no Bitcoin transactions will be finalized. This means that not only will Bitcoin payments fail to be sent and received but there will be no new Bitcoins created.

Bitcoin miners know that there are only a limited amount of Bitcoins available, and as time passes they will all be competing for a dwindling number. They just leave their Bitcoin mining computers running 24 hours a day to keep verifying and confirming transactions and trying to earn those elusive Bitcoins.

No Trust Required

The design of Bitcoin and the underlying blockchain technology is such that no trust is required. It uses heavy encryption techniques to keep everything safe, hence the name "cryptocurrency".

There is no need for human trust in the Bitcoin network because it operates on tried and tested computer algorithms. It is virtually impossible to cheat the Bitcoin network because it is a public environment. It would take a ton of computing power to break down all of the encryption, even if that were possible. So it makes more sense to use this kind of computing power to mine the Bitcoin network instead.

Your identity is protected on the Bitcoin network. All of your Bitcoin transactions are verified using a private and public key. You use your private key as your "digital signature" in your Bitcoin transactions and network users can verify this by using your public key. Both of these keys are encrypted so you can only use the public key if the correct private key is used.

Public and private keys are very important for you to understand as a cryptocurrency investor. A public key is tied to a public address where you can deposit cryptocurrencies. You can use your public address to broadcast so that you can receive payments from other peers.

Your private key is not to for sharing with anyone as it is essentially the password to protect your funds. This private key links to your public key for added security. Your private key is how your balance is determined through the Bitcoin network.

The public and private key system has two major advantages:

1. It is virtually impossible for cyber criminals to steal your identity and make fraudulent transactions
2. You can be completely anonymous on the Bitcoin network if that is useful for you

Now you know how Bitcoin really works. In the next chapter we will look at the various ways that you can acquire Bitcoins.

Acquiring Bitcoins

With the growing popularity of Bitcoin came a number of different methods for acquiring them. In this chapter we will explain some of the most common methods for acquiring Bitcoins to bolster your investments.

Purchase Bitcoins

This is obviously the most simple and straightforward way to acquire Bitcoins. All you need to do is to use an exchange website such as Coinbase.com and in most cases you will be able to buy Bitcoins using your native currency.

Some cryptocurrency exchanges have country restrictions so you need to do your homework here to ensure that you can purchase in your country. There are some countries that have actually banned the buying and selling of Bitcoin so if this applies to you then you will need to find a creative way around this which is beyond the scope of this guide.

Sometimes a single Bitcoin can be worth around $10,000 so to make Bitcoin investment available to all most exchanges will sell fractions. In fact a Bitcoin can be divided into 100 million units. Each of these units is called a "Satoshi" after the founder of Bitcoin.

We will give you our view on using cryptocurrency exchanges in the next chapter when we explain what you need to get started with Bitcoin investment. For now here is our view of the best cryptocurrency exchanges for Bitcoin:

Coinbase is probably the best known cryptocurrency exchange. If you have used a stock trading platform before, then the interface of Coinbase will make sense to you. You can fund your Coinbase account using bank transfers from the US and eventually with credit cards. You can exchange either US dollars or cryptocurrency that you already have for Bitcoin.

Each trade that you make with Coinbase will incur a small fee, which at the time of writing this guide was 1.5% for Bitcoin purchases and 0.25% for transfers. The biggest issue with Coinbase among the cryptocurrency community is that you have to provide a lot of personal information.

Sometimes Coinbase will close accounts for a variety of reasons. There are people that believe the website has a tie in with some major banks and will not use it because of this. Coinbase does everything by the book as far as that is possible. This means that there is much less chance of site closure than with other cryptocurrency exchanges.

In 2011 **Kraken** was formed for the buying and selling cryptocurrencies. You can buy and sell Bitcoin as well as other popular cryptocurrencies on Kraken. A good feature of Kraken is that it has a number of currency pairings such as USD with Bitcoin, and it supports many more fiat currencies than Coinbase. The fees are lower, too.

Kraken has a very good reputation in the cryptocurrency community. If you are interested in trading Bitcoin there are a number of good features such as margin trading.

The biggest criticism of Kraken is that the platform can be counterintuitive and confusing at times. As a newcomer to Bitcoin investing, we do not recommend that you use Kraken first. Once you have some experience under your belt then you may consider migrating this this platform.

Poloniex is a cryptocurrency exchange based in the United States that has a high volume of trades. The biggest problem with Poloniex is that it doesn't accept fiat currency. Once you have some Bitcoin you can use this exchange for trades as there is margin trading for more than 90 pairs.

Poloniex has very low fees, typically below 0.25%. Unfortunately it has a pretty bad rap for customer support and it is not that easy to withdraw funds from the exchange. They can also close your account for any reason which is not good.

Bittrex is a no fiat currency trading platform. Bittrex holds most of its funds offline in a similar way to Coinbase making it more secure. The customer service provided by Bittrex is very good, but it is not as beginner-friendly as some of the other exchanges.

A lot of beginners start with Coinbase, but you will have to provide a lot of personal details with this exchange. If this doesn't bother you, then it is a good choice. There are many cryptocurrency exchanges available. We recommend that you do your homework to see which exchanges support your country and suit you the best.

Cash exchanges are an alternative to cryptocurrency exchanges. Here you can pay with cash for your Bitcoins and you will trade directly with the owner of the Bitcoins. A good example is **LocalBitcoins.com** where you can trade in over 7,700 cities and 248 countries. You can buy and sell Bitcoins using this cash exchange.

Another alternative cash exchange for the buying and selling of Bitcoins is Wall of Coins. Most cash exchanges do not have expensive fees but sometimes you have to pay fees for successful trading. We recommend that you use a cash exchange that provides an escrow service to protect your funds.

Trade Other Cryptocurrencies for Bitcoin

If you happen to have other cryptocurrencies you can trade these for Bitcoins pretty easily. One of the easiest places to do this is at ShapeShift.io. An account is not necessary to make a small trade.

All you need to do to exchange your other cryptocurrencies for Bitcoin is to enter the amount for trading or conversion, add your Bitcoin address and the refund address for your cryptocurrency. It just takes a few minutes to exchange for Bitcoins.

Get Paid In Bitcoin

It is easy to be paid in Bitcoins. All that you need is your own wallet for Bitcoin and you can receive payments. You can get a free Bitcoin wallet at **Coinbase** or at **Blockchain.com**. It just takes an email address to get your wallet.

Once your wallet is set up you can receive payments in Bitcoin. You can generate a QR code and then send this to the person that you will receive the Bitcoin payment from. There are a number of ways that you can be paid in Bitcoins and here are some of the most popular methods:

Perform Work for Bitcoins

You will find a number of different types of work that you can perform in exchange for Bitcoins. A lot of these are online and popular with freelancers across the world. When you are paid with Bitcoin you do not have to wait for a bank transfer which can take days to reach your account. You can have your Bitcoins in minutes.

Employers or customers like paying in Bitcoins too as they do not have to pay high transaction fees associated with bank transfers especially if their workers live in another country.

Sell Products and Services for Bitcoin

Whether you own a conventional brick and mortar store or an online store you can receive payments from customers in Bitcoin. With the growth of Bitcoin, there are bound to be customers that hold Bitcoin and see it as a forward thinking and convenient way to make payments.

It is easier for customers as well as they can just make the payment from their Bitcoin wallet. Of course you will receive the payment in Bitcoin pretty fast too. This is a win-win for you and your customers.

If you have an online store there are a number of scripts or plugins you can use to accept payments via Bitcoin. You must ensure that you set everything up correctly because you don't want your payments ending up in someone else's wallet.

For a brick and mortar business you can start accepting payments via Bitcoin simply by printing the QR code of your Bitcoin wallet for customers to use. A customer can use their smart phone to scan the QR code and then make the payment.

Be sure to tell all of your customers that you accept Bitcoin as a means of payment. Add your details to Coinmap.org which will let Bitcoin users know that you take it as a form of payment. There are similar websites you can post to as well.

Why not use Bitcoin as a way of receiving tips? This is easy to do online by setting up a Bitcoin payment gateway. If you have a blog and provide useful content for example, some of your readers will be happy to send you a tip using Bitcoin.

Websites that Pay in Bitcoin

There are many websites available that will pay you in Bitcoins (usually small fractions) for completing certain tasks. Some of these tasks include:

- Completing surveys
- Downloading mobile apps
- Watching videos
- Play games online
- Click on ads
- Sign up for trial offers
- Shop online
- Answer questions
- Refer friends

Some of the websites just need the address of your Bitcoin wallet. Others will require you to create an account with them. You can perform most of these tasks in minutes and earn fractions of Bitcoins. If you value your time then you may not be interested in doing this.

Bitcoin Faucets

Most people have not heard of Bitcoin faucets. What they do is to give away fractions of Bitcoins for free at specific times. This drives a ton of traffic as lots of people want these free Bitcoin fractions and sometimes these faucets take a long time to load.

There are some Bitcoin faucets that just give away Satoshis. Other faucets require that you complete some small tasks to earn your Satoshis. Before you get too excited by Bitcoin faucets, you need to know that they can steal a great deal of your time for fractions of Bitcoins.

Bitcoin Mining

We have mentioned how important Bitcoin miners are to the Bitcoin network. If miners didn't exist then there would be no transactions or new Bitcoins created. Bitcoin miners can find Bitcoins which is their reward for their efforts.

When Bitcoin first launched it was fairly common for Bitcoin miners to receive 50 Bitcoins when they mined a single block. But as every block was mined the number of available Bitcoins for rewards diminished.

Now you will get a lot less Bitcoins for mining. However, with the prices rising some people still see this as a worthwhile task. But Bitcoin mining is not an easy thing to do. You need some powerful computers to be a successful Bitcoin miner.

It is now a lot more difficult to mine new blocks and solving the complex cryptographic functions is really tough. There is also a lot of competition in Bitcoin mining now making the task even more difficult.

These days most Blockchain miners work together in pools, and they split any rewards that they receive for their efforts based on the amount of work that their computers have done. It is not cheap to participate in Bitcoin mining these days. You need powerful computers to solve the cryptographic functions.

Forget about using a high end desktop to perform Bitcoin mining. You will have to invest in some serious hardware even to join a Bitcoin mining pool. It is recommended that you use an ASIC chip to have any success with Bitcoin mining. These chips and high end computers also consume a lot of power.

The other thing that you need is knowledge. To setup a Bitcoin mining system you will have to pay experts to do this. We are not saying that it is not possible to be successful with Bitcoin mining over the long term, but you will have to make a significant investment to get started.

Let's get further clarification from the source of all geek wisdom, ***The Big Bang Theory:***

Season 11, Episode 9: The Bitcoin Entanglement
Airdate November 30, 2017

Sheldon starts a conversation on Bitcoins that are now worth $5,000 apiece. Seven years ago, the guys (minus Sheldon) mined some Bitcoins using Howard's old laptop. He describes how one must solve complex mathematical problems to earn the crypto. The guys are spend a whole night trying to accumulate the Bitcoins, but Sheldon doesn't, because he is worried about the tax implications.

Howard remembers the mining, and now wants to use the stash to fund infant daughter Halley's college fund. Howard doesn't find the Bitcoins on any of the computers. The three remember they finished up using Leonard's laptop, which has since been loaned to someone else. Recovering the laptop, they still can't find the Bitcoins. Sheldon confesses he downloaded these and shifted them to Leonard's Batman flash drive keychain as a prank. Leonard tells him that he lost that key chain years ago. In a flashback, Stuart finds the keychain on the floor of the comic book store, and unaware of the value of the contents, erases it and puts it out for sale.

MORAL: Don't be Howard. Secure your wallet and key codes.

Choosing the Right Bitcoin Wallet

Although the blockchain technology that underpins Bitcoin is very secure, one of the biggest weak points with Bitcoin is storage. Because Bitcoins have risen significantly in value over the years you will not be surprised to know that the number of cyber criminal's intent on stealing Bitcoins has risen too.

And these people are getting smarter and smarter. They are creating bots that will scan online Bitcoin wallets and try and remove the Bitcoins in them. There have been several reports about cyber criminals emptying cryptocurrency exchange wallets over the years and the wallet holders never seeing their Bitcoins again.

We want you to be shocked and concerned by this. If you are going to be a successful Bitcoin investor then you need to hang on to your Bitcoins! It is essential that you keep your Bitcoins safe, and fortunately there is a lot you can do to ensure this. The type of Bitcoin wallet that you choose is crucial to the security of your Bitcoins.

It is all about keeping your private key safe. Inside of your wallet your Bitcoins have an associated address which consists of your private key and public key. The public key is the actual address of the Bitcoin and your private key is the password that unlocks those Bitcoins. It is essential that you keep your private key safe.

If a cyber criminal gets their hands on your private key then they can transfer all of your Bitcoins to other accounts. And you know that once a Bitcoin transaction is verified and confirmed then there is no turning back.

People that are unlucky enough to have Bitcoins stolen from their wallets just have to accept it and get on with their lives. You just cannot do anything to get your Bitcoins back. So let's take a look at the different types of wallets and how you can provide the maximum protection for your private key.

Online Bitcoin Wallets

There is no easier way to get started with Bitcoin investing than to setup an online wallet. You can setup a free Bitcoin online wallet even if you have no Bitcoins right now. Cryptocurrency exchanges like Coinbase will provide you with an online wallet and you can get one at Blockchain.com as well.

When you are just starting out then an online wallet is a good thing to use. But you would not want to keep a sizeable Bitcoin inventory in an online wallet. Yes it is great that you can access your online wallet from anywhere in the world but so can thieves and cyber criminals!

An online wallet is a "hot" wallet because all you need to access it is an Internet connection. The problem is that most online wallets end up storing your private keys on their servers and if these get hacked you can say goodbye to your Bitcoins.

The other issue is that servers can and do have technical problems and if they suffer a catastrophic issue then your private keys could disappear forever. Some online wallet platforms will limit or suspend accounts for terms of service infractions and you may even have your account shut down permanently and you lose your private keys.

We strongly recommend that if you have a significant amount of Bitcoins that you move them to a cold wallet which is offline. Don't take the chance of not being in control of your Bitcoins.

Online wallets are not all bad. Yes there are security and other risks but if you intend to make frequent Bitcoin transactions then they are useful. You can hold a small amount of Bitcoins in your online wallet for those regular transactions and then move the rest to a more secure wallet.

Mobile Bitcoin Wallets

A mobile wallet is another form of hot online wallet. With a mobile wallet you can access it using your mobile device when you connect to the Internet. If you have a smartphone or tablet that you take around with you wherever you go then this is a very convenient type of Bitcoin wallet.

With a mobile wallet you can make Bitcoin payments to a vendor either online or offline. If you have a Blockchain.com or Coinbase online wallet then there is a mobile counterpart synchronized to your main wallet.

Despite being very convenient there are issues with mobile wallets. Cyber criminals and hackers can still get hold of your private keys if they are saved on your mobile device or remote servers.

A lot of people lose their mobile phones or have them stolen. Also a lot of mobile phones suffer damage. If you don't make copies of your private keys then you could potentially lose all of your Bitcoins in these scenarios.

To get the best use out of a mobile wallet we recommend that you transfer just what you need to it from a more secure wallet. Then if you lose your phone or it becomes unusable you will still have your private keys safely stored in the secure wallet.

Desktop Computer Bitcoin Wallet

Another choice for you is the desktop wallet. It is a much safer choice than an online or mobile wallet as you download an app for your computer or laptop and you store your private keys in it.

One of the most popular desktop wallets is **Bitcoin Core.** In our opinion this is not the most practical choice. The reason is that Bitcoin Core will actually download the complete blockchain, so you will need at least 150 GB of spare disk space to make this work.

The good news is that there are alternative desktop wallets that you can use which do not require you to download the blockchain for Bitcoin. Instead they use simple payment verification (SPV) technology. Some good examples are:

- **Bitcoin Core**   **https://bitcoin.org/en/bitcoin-core**
- **Electrum**   **https://electrum.org**
- **Armory**   **https://bitcomarmory.com**
- **Bither**   **https://blither.net**

Desktop wallets are simple to use and so much safer than online or mobile wallets. With a desktop wallet you can disconnect your computer from the Internet to prevent hackers from accessing your private keys.

While it is true that a desktop wallet does not have the convenience of an online wallet you will have control over your private keys. You can also make a backup in case your laptop or computer is stolen or becomes inoperable.

Paper Bitcoin Wallet

It may seem a strange thing to store your Bitcoins on paper as they do not seem to be a very good technological match, but paper wallets are another "cold storage" option, as it is impossible for even the most competent cyber criminals to hack a piece of paper in your desk or safe deposit box!

Of course, if you do not take care of a paper wallet in the real world, then people can steal it. If you choose this option, then don't leave it lying around. You also need to protect paper wallets from damage as well so use a water resistant container to store them.

A paper wallet definitely does not have the convenience of an online wallet, but they are a lot safer. All you need to do is to print off your private and public keys and store the paper somewhere secure such as a safety deposit box.

Paper wallets are a good long term option. You can store large amount of Bitcoins in your paper wallet and then have a few available in an online wallet for regular transactions. It is definitely one to consider.

Hardware Bitcoin Wallet

Most Bitcoin experts will tell you that the most secure types of Bitcoin wallets are hardware wallets. We agree, and if you are serious about Bitcoin investing then we strongly recommend that you invest in a hardware wallet. They are not cheap, but they are worth it.

The majority of hardware wallets will enable you to store other cryptocurrencies as well as Bitcoin. A hardware wallet is usually in the form of a USB stick which you just insert into your computer when you want to make a Bitcoin transaction. Once you are done, just remove the hardware wallet and then store it safely.

A really good security feature with hardware wallets is the ability to create private keys offline. You can carry your hardware wallet around with you wherever you go without the worry of having your private keys stolen.

It is really easy to setup and use a hardware wallet. With most hardware wallets you can set a password and PIN code and even add recovery seed words to authenticate access and to recover any stored Bitcoins if you lose your hardware wallet or it stops working.

We recommend that you write down all of your security details for your hardware wallet just in case you forget them. Hide these details in a place that only you know about. If these details fall into the wrong hands, you can lose all of your Bitcoins.

There is no chance of a hardware wallet being hacked, so the only thing you have to do is to keep a backup of your security details in a safe place.

At the end of the day you will probably want to use a combination of different wallets as you become a more serious Bitcoin investor. Hardware and paper wallets are the best choice for long term storage. You can use a desktop wallet for medium term storage and an online wallet for those frequent short term Bitcoin transactions.

You may have heard how others have purchased Bitcoins in the past and ended up selling them for a huge profit. It is still possible and there is no reason why you can't do this too.

There are certainly experienced Bitcoin traders out there that make a lot of money from their trades. They may not be successful with every trade but overall they make consistent profits. The thing is that trading Bitcoins successfully is not an easy thing to do. You really have to be prepared.

It is not impossible for someone just starting out with Bitcoin to be successful. But you have to be financially and mentally ready for this. Bitcoin trading is all about high risk and high reward. The key to success is to buy at low prices and then sell at higher prices. While this is obvious it is not that easy to do.

A lot of newcomers to Bitcoin trading end up panicking when they are making trades. After all, they are dealing with digital currency that is worth thousands of dollars. Panic levels will rise even more if you are using your savings or your pension fund to trade!

Strategies for Bitcoin Trading

If you are really interested in Bitcoin trading then the first thing that you need to realize is that you need to use common sense and maintain self-control. Don't go into it thinking that you are going to make a ton of money in a day. If you get too greedy then you are very likely to fail.

You need to learn everything that you can about Bitcoin trading before you start to do it for real. Knowledge is great but there is nothing like experiencing how Bitcoin trading works in the real world.

To give yourself a good start with Bitcoin trading sign up with a cryptocurrency exchange that will allow you to use a demo account to experience how things work in the real world. You will see real time prices for Bitcoin and it will help you to get used to the Bitcoin trading interface.

You Need a Trading Plan

Successful Bitcoin trading relies on having a good strategy in place. Sure you might get lucky with your first few trades, but sooner or later your luck will run out and this can be very expensive.

One of the biggest mistakes that newcomers to Bitcoin trading make is that they follow the news, see that a lot of other people are making Bitcoin trades and this compels them to do the same thing. Experienced traders like this because it will force the Bitcoin price up and they can profit from previous purchases.

Don't follow trends blindly. Create a plan that defines the price that you should purchase Bitcoins for and the price that you should sell them at to realize the profit that you want. If you stick to a plan like this then you will significantly reduce the risk of panicking if you suddenly see prices fall.

Practice with Small Amounts

When you are starting out with Bitcoin trading only invest small amounts with trades. This is all part of your learning curve and early training. No matter how good an opportunity seems resist the temptation to go "all in".

Use your demo account to perform a lot of trades before you start spending real money. If you clean out your demo account then this is not a big deal but losing all of your real money is completely devastating.

Keep Your Emotions in Check

The thought of losing money can be really alarming to you. We have told you many times in this guide that Bitcoin is volatile and in one day the price can go down by a significant amount. The good thing is that the price can rise significantly in no time at all as well.

You must keep your emotions in check if you want to be successful with Bitcoin trading. Thinking logically will always be the best strategy. Never let your emotions determine which Bitcoin trades you should or shouldn't make.

It is understandable that you will be excited about the opportunities that Bitcoin trading offers. But we strongly recommend that you take this a step at a time and learn everything that you can about trading.

Use a few demo accounts to practice with before you start investing real money. The more accustomed you are with the trading environment the better. If you make mistakes with your demo account work out what went wrong and avoid making the same mistake in the future.

Investment Strategies

In an earlier chapter we provided you with a lowdown on Bitcoin investing. In this chapter we will look at some of the real life Bitcoin investment strategies that are working well for some savvy investors.

Many people are jumping on the Bitcoin investment bandwagon nowadays because of the price rises but most of these people fail because they are ill prepared. They do not have the advantage of reading a guide like this to help them like you do.

Throughout this guide we have made no secret of the fact that Bitcoin is a volatile digital currency and it goes up and down in value on a regular basis. That is why we recommend that you adopt a long term approach to your Bitcoin investing so that if the price does drop you give it time to recover.

So here we will take a more in depth look at some of the "real life" methods that successful Bitcoin investors use to make a profit.

The Dollar Cost Averaging Method

This is the best Bitcoin investment method for beginners, because it removes the need to enter the Bitcoin market when the timing is right. A lot of novice Bitcoin investors spend a lot of time and stress waiting for the price of Bitcoin to fall to the right level.

When you use the dollar cost averaging method for your Bitcoin investing, you will spread your risk over a time period. All you need to do is make purchases at regular intervals and then hold them in your secure wallet.

Here is an example of how this works. Let's say that each week you can spare $100 to invest in Bitcoin. You make a purchase every week for $100 and some weeks you will receive more Bitcoins for your money and others you will get less.

There is no need for you to study Bitcoin price charts for hours. All you need to do is have the discipline to make those $100 purchases every week. You don't have to wait around for the right price drops just make your purchase anyway.

When you use the dollar averaging method, you will find that your profits average out when you decide to sell. You might not achieve huge profits using this method, but if you sell when the Bitcoin price is high then you will still make a good return.

Investing a Lump Sum into Bitcoins

This method is definitely not one for the faint of heart, but we want to cover all bases here. When you invest a lump sum in Bitcoins you will purchase them at a specific price point. There is an element of risk when you do this.

Let's assume that you have $50,000 to invest. Naturally you want to get as many Bitcoins as possible for your investment. In order to have the best chance of doing this, you have no choice but to wait until the Bitcoin price goes down.

There is no other alternative here. You must wait and time your entry into the Bitcoin market as well as you can. The problem is that, in practice, the price of Bitcoin fluctuates very often, so predicting the next price dip is really tough to do.

If you have a lump sum to invest right now, we wouldn't advise that you start with this. It takes experience to make a good judgment of the right price dip. Even the experts get this wrong sometimes.

When you are new to Bitcoin investing and want to invest a lump sum, you may see a price dip and then think to yourself "If I just hang on for a while it may go down even more" or "What if the price never reaches my low point?"

The same scenario applies to selling your lump sum investment. How do you know the best price to sell your Bitcoins? It may be very difficult to sell at the price that you need to make the profit you planned.

If you sell too soon and the price goes up even more, then you will criticize yourself. Think what you could have done with all of that extra profit! Obviously a lump sum investment will provide you with a much higher profit than the dollar cost averaging method if you get the timing just right.

Bitcoin Investing Hedge Fund

There are cryptocurrency hedge funds available that include Bitcoin. This could be a good alternative for you if you do not want to do your homework learning about Bitcoin investment strategies. The biggest drawback with any hedge fund is the often expensive performance and management fees.

Cryptocurrency hedge funds will insist that you pay the management fee upfront. Usually these fees are in the region of 2% of your investment, so if you want to invest $100,000 then you are going to have to pay around $2,000 as a management fee which leaves you with $98,000 for investing in cryptocurrencies.

You will be appointed a hedge fund manager and they work on a profits percentage basis. This can be as high as 20%, so if you were able to secure a $40,000 profit from your investment then you will have to pay $8,000 to your hedge fund manager.

These figures may startle you, and cryptocurrency hedge funds are not going to be everyone's idea of a good thing. If you want to have totally hands off investing which can make big profits for you, you will end up paying for that convenience. Also remember the hedge fund manager loses *potential* income if your investment crashes, while you lose *real* money. I watched one client lose his million-dollar retirement fund by relying on hedge fund investment managers, so I tend to be very suspicious of that entire field.

Avoiding Scams

Although Bitcoin is certainly not a scam, there are plenty of people out there that will try and scam you out of your precious Bitcoins. Like any other high value commodity some people will do everything that they can to get their hands on Bitcoins. So in this chapter we will look at some of the most common scams that you need to avoid.

Fake Bitcoin Exchanges

We would always recommend that you use a cryptocurrency exchange that has an established reputation and have been operating for a few years. In this guide we have told you about Coinbase, Kraken, Poloniex and Bittrex. There are others too such as Cex.io, Bitstamp.net and Changelly.com.

There are so many cryptocurrency exchanges available today that it would be impossible for use to vouch for any of them. You need to conduct your own due diligence here and find out the history and look for reviews from users.

If you see an exchange offering rates that are just too good to be true then be very suspicious. Unfortunately there are fake exchanges that look like the real thing and then when you try to trade with them they will steal your Bitcoins and you will never see them again.

These fake exchanges prey on newcomers to the Bitcoin space. They offer the opportunity to purchase Bitcoins for up to 20% lower than you would see on reputable sites like Coinbase. Unfortunately some new people fall for this scam – you know better now!

Another sign of a fake exchange is where they offer to purchase your Bitcoins from you at a higher than average price and then send you the amount in US dollars to your PayPal account. This will never happen and they will just steal your Bitcoins.

Phishing Scams

These are performed using email. The aim is to get the login details for your online wallet. So you will receive an email from a domain name that looks like Coinbase.com for example that is not from the genuine site. It might be from Coinsbase.com pretending to be Coinbase.com or they use other tricks.

If you fall for this kind of phishing scam and use your Coinbase.com login details to log into the fake website then the scammers then have your information and can login to your Coinbase account, lock you out of your own account and steal all your Bitcoins!

Malware Scams

These are nasty. You will be asked to click a link in an email or on a website that will download malware on your computer without you knowing it. Usually the malware is a keylogger which will record everything that you type and send this back to the scammers. So if you type in your Coinbase username and password this will be shared with the thieves.

Never click on any links in emails or on websites that you are not 100% sure about. If you notice something being downloaded then stop it immediately.

Ponzi Scams

If someone offered you a guaranteed return on your investment then you would be interested right? Well here's the thing – nobody can offer you this kind of guarantee with cryptocurrencies. There is no such thing as a risk free investment.

Bitcoin and other cryptocurrencies are volatile by their very nature. If someone tells you that they can guarantee a daily 10% return on investment they are a scammer. A Ponzi scheme pays off the early members with the investments made by new members. It has been going on for years and so many people fall for new ones.

The best way to avoid Ponzi scheme scams is to always bear in mind that if it seems too good to be true then it probably isn't.

Mining Scams

There is a lot of interest in Bitcoin mining. Cloud mining is a concept where you do not have to invest heavily in the necessary high level computer hardware for Bitcoin mining. Simply join a group and the mining is done for you. Of course you will need to pay for this privilege.

While there are legitimate cloud mining programs there are a number of scammers as well. Take a good look at the website to see if they have a secure https domain and also search for reviews about the company on search engines.

We don't recommend that you get into Bitcoin mining when you are starting out. If you do like the idea of cloud mining then you must do your homework otherwise you run the risk of scammers taking your money for nothing in return.

Best Investing Practices

We want you to be a successful Bitcoin investor. Although nothing is ever guaranteed when investing in cryptocurrencies, there are certain practices that you can follow that will maximize your chances of success.

1. Understand how Bitcoin works

We have given you all the information that you need in this guide to understand how Bitcoin really works. You need to know the principles of blockchain and how Bitcoin trades are made. Don't get caught up in the technicalities but make sure that you have a firm understanding of Bitcoin before you make any trades.

2. Go for Long Term Investment

You may have heard a lot of stories about traders who make money from Bitcoin trades every day. Some of these may be true but these people have a lot of experience and know what they are doing! Go for a long term investment strategy (buy and hold) instead to battle against the volatility of Bitcoin.

3. Be Wallet Secure

We devoted an entire chapter on the different types of wallets for Bitcoin and their security issues. Online wallets are the least secure and hardware wallets are the most secure. For convenience it works the other way around with online or "hot" wallets being the most convenient and offline or "cold" wallets being the least convenient.

Bitcoins are very valuable so you need to have the right wallets to protect them. If you are going to trade regularly then just keep enough Bitcoins in an online wallet to do this and keep the rest in your cold wallet. If thieves get hold of your private keys then you can say goodbye to your Bitcoins.

4. Use Reputable Exchanges to buy and sell Bitcoins

Due to the high value of Bitcoins there are plenty of thieves and scammers out there who want to steal yours from you. Only use a reputable cryptocurrency exchange such as Coinbase or Kraken to buy and sell your Bitcoins.

Always check out a cryptocurrency exchange thoroughly. Do they have a track record? Are there user reviews? If you can't find these things then look for another exchange. If an exchange is making promises of Bitcoin deals that seem too good to be true then move on.

5. Watch Bitcoin Trends

It is always a good idea to keep an eye on the price fluctuations of Bitcoin. Use tools like Bitcoin Wisdom and Cryptowatch to stay in the loop. This is especially important if you are thinking about investing a lump sum into Bitcoin. You want to buy at the lowest price and sell at the highest price.

6. Avoid Bitcoin Trading Initially

Once you get more experience as a Bitcoin investor then you can try your hand at Bitcoin trading. We do not recommend that you start trading straight away. You need to learn a great deal about Bitcoin pricing and be able to effectively control your emotions to trade successfully.

There are demo accounts available that you can use to practice Bitcoin trading. Use these to the full and learn from any mistakes that you make before you start using real money to trade Bitcoins.

7. Accept that Bitcoin is Volatile and High Risk

Bitcoin is a highly volatile digital currency. This means that there are opportunities to make significant gains and the risk of losing a lot of money too. You need to accept this and always bear it in mind to be a successful Bitcoin investor.

8. Avoid Scams

Unfortunately there are many cryptocurrency scams. Bitcoins are very valuable and thieves will do everything that they can to steal them from you. Watch out for fake exchanges, phishing in emails and too good to be true Ponzi schemes.

9. Avoid Bitcoin Mining

Do not get involved in Bitcoin mining when you are starting out. You will need to make a significant investment in high-end computer equipment to have any chance of success, and it just makes more sense to use this money to purchase Bitcoins instead.

SECTION III: Super Simple PLAN B

So you've examined your motives and goals, and have decided:

- Simpler is better.

- You don't really want to make or accept payment in Bitcoin.

- You don't really want to make semi-anonymous global transactions.

- You don't really want to mess with wallets and faucets and key.

- What you really want is to buy Bitcoins or other cryptocurrencies to own something that will gain value and be easily liquid when you want to cash out.

- In other words, you consider Bitcoins to be another investment asset that will rise or fall in value on the global market.

- You've heard that Bitcoin, which is worth about $9,500 as I write this, could be worth $1,000,000 to $5,000,000 in the next five years, and you want a piece without jumping through computer geek hoops.

Us too!

The answer we've found is an online brokerage called Robinhood.com .

1. **You will need a working bank account with online access.**

2. **Set up your free, no-fee, online brokerage account.**
   Go to **share.robinhood.com/brianw2647** and sign up. Keep your user name and password in a safe place!

3. **Link your brokerage account to one or more of your bank accounts.**
   The app will offer you several major banks. If your bank is listed, click the button. If your bank is NOT listed, select "Bank Not Listed". You will be asked for the name of the bank, routing number, and account number. All of these are on your checks. The app will verify by making two small deposits in your account within three days. When this happens, you must enter those amounts into the app under Account >Banking > Verify.

4. **Fund your brokerage account.**
Deposit as much as you like from your bank account. I started with ten dollars.

5. **Draw a card for a free gift stock.**
The app will show you an animation to pick one of three shuffling cards. Each one is a different stock share. The one you pick will be put into your account portfolio. All are good, and some are exceptional! FREE means it's pure profit, so smile.

6. **Begin referring clients.**
You should have received a referral link in the "share.robinhood.com/" format above. When others sign up using that link, you will eventually have a chance to draw for another gift stock share. (If you have completed all the steps, you have put me in line for more gift stock, so thank you! Win-Win!) Now we start the fun part: market research, due diligence, developing investment strategies. Looking for rapid growth? Stability? Dividends? Not sure yet?

7. **Sign up for Robinhood Cryptocurrency.****
If there's a backlog, it may take a few days to be approved. You must then read and approve the terms of use.

Here's where it get a little tricky. RH bills itself as a no-fee brokerage, and that's true for stocks. However, the crypto side works a little differently. There will be some fees involved, which are spelled out in the terms. But unlike a personal Bitcoin wallet, you do not actually own the Bitcoins. Analogy: Robinhood owns a large cookie jar of Bitcoins, and agrees to put your name on some of them. When you cash them out, there will be a fee. All you can actually do with them is cash them out into your Robinhood "Cash" account, and from there make further purchases or transfer them to your bank account. You agree to trust Robinhood to keep their word.

So while you don't have to worry about losing your Batman thumb-drive keyring and the fortune encoded on it, you give up the unique functionality of cryptocurrency for convenience and security.

It's a deal that has worked well for me, but decide for yourself if you're happier with Plan A.

8. Research.

You will have to do your own research. Your money, your investment, your responsibility. There's plenty of up-to-date information you can search on Google and YouTube. These sources will often conflict. As you gain experience, you will develop discernment. Caution is recommended.

** At this printing, it is not clear who owns the keys to your Bitcoin if you buy via Robinhood. Do you actually own the Bitcoin or not? What you instead own is Robinhood's promise that when you go to sell your Bitcoin, they will give you the US dollar equivalent, so you can't actually move "your" Bitcoin from Robinhood into a cold storage wallet. If you don't own your private keys, you do not own Bitcoin. If you think about it, this goes against the reason why Bitcoin exists. Bitcoin is supposed to be sovereign money that you alone have 100% complete control over, and if someone else has the ownership of your money, does that really make it yours? This is now analogous to hard currency, in which you hold an IOU from the government to pay you in gold or silver on demand, but you do not actually have possession of the metals.

If you are comfortable buying a promise from Robinhood – which is a very reputable firm with a great track record – then by all means, this is a great way to get started.

To qualify to buy crypto on Robinhood, you accept a 20 page user agreement, Under Subsection C, you'll see rebates and pass on of fees. No matter how you obtain or transfer cryptocurrencies, there are fees. Do your own due diligence so you aren't surprised by these when they are charged.

Two comments from Robinhood as of July 2020:

"We don't support transfers of your existing cryptocurrency assets or wallets into your Robinhood Crypto account. Our primary concern is preventing the proceeds from illegal activity from being used for transactions on Robinhood

Crypto. We'll be sure to update you if and when this type of transfer becomes available."

"We don't currently provide you with access to your wallet or your wallet address. You own the cryptocurrency assets in your account, and you can buy or sell them at any time. We're evaluating features to allow you to safely transfer coins to and from Robinhood, and we'll update you when these features are available."

CHECKLISTS

PLAN A

Resource #1
- Write down your goals for Bitcoin investing
- Monitor the price of Bitcoin using CoinDesk.com
- Learn about the previous cycles of Bitcoin to identify swings
- Use Cryptowat.ch and BitcoinWisdom.com to monitor Bitcoin trends
- Goal: Prepare yourself with all of the information that you need for successful Bitcoin investment. To make the highest profits you need to buy at the lowest price and sell at the highest price.

Resource #2
- Look at a number of cryptocurrency exchanges for the best deals
- Check out the reputations of any exchange you are considering and also look for reviews
- Look for cash exchanges where you can easily and securely trade Bitcoins for cash
- If you want to work for Bitcoins then check which freelancing websites will pay you this way
- Look into offering your customers a Bitcoin payment option for your offline or online store
- Look for websites that pay in Bitcoin for performing small tasks
- Look for **Bitcoin Faucets** that give away Bitcoins
- Goal: There are different ways that you can acquire Bitcoins so consider the options that best suit you.

Resource #3
- Get a free online wallet from a reputable exchange or at Blockchain.com
- If you use a mobile device then checkout online wallets that are mobile friendly
- Investigate the different desktop wallet options for medium security
- If you want to use a paper wallet then consider where you will store this – a safety deposit box?
- Look at the different types of hardware wallet available and choose one that best suits your requirements and budget
- Goal: You must have a secure wallet for most of your Bitcoins. Never leave your Bitcoins in an exchange online wallet as you could lose them all.

Resource #4

- Look for cryptocurrency trading websites that provide a free demo account
- Investigate how experienced traders make profits from Bitcoin
- Create a plan for Bitcoin trading and stick to it
- Goal: Bitcoin day trading is difficult but it can be very profitable. Learn as much as you can and use a demo account for a while before you start to use real money for Bitcoin trades

Resource #5

- Identify cryptocurrency exchanges that provide you with what you want e.g. exchanging fiat currency for Bitcoins
- Check all of the potential cryptocurrency exchanges for good reviews and a good track record. Use forums to identify any scam exchanges.
- Decide on how much you can afford to invest on a regular basis using the dollar cost averaging method
- If you want to invest a lump sum into Bitcoin then spend time learning how to check trends and identify when you can buy at the lowest prices
- Do some research into cryptocurrency hedge funds and see if this is something that appeals to you
- Goal: You need to choose a Bitcoin investment strategy that suits you best.

PLAN B

- **Set up your free, no-fee, online brokerage account.**
  Go to **share.robinhood.com/brianw2647** and sign up. Keep your user name and password in a safe place!
- **Link your brokerage account to one or more of your bank accounts and verify test deposits.**
- **Fund your brokerage account.**
- **Draw a card for a free gift stock.**
- **Begin referring clients to earn more stock shares.**
- **Sign up for Robinhood Cryptocurrency.**
- **Purchases Bitcoin or another cryptocurrency of your choice.**

Conclusion

If you have read this guide carefully, you now have a strong foundation in Bitcoin and can take this forward to start making sound investments. This is just the start for you so we urge you to track the trends with Bitcoin and to keep abreast of all new developments with this cryptocurrency.

There have been fortunes made through Bitcoin investing and trading. But it is not a get rich overnight situation. You need to develop an investment plan and only make investments that you can afford. Initially we strongly recommend that you approach Bitcoin investing as a long term investment.

With more and more businesses realizing the power of Bitcoin you will be able to use yours in more places to make purchases in the near future. If you have a business yourself then we strongly recommend that you provide your customers with the choice of making Bitcoin payments.

If you are concerned about the future of Bitcoin then there is no need for this. It is growing and here to stay. The fact that you can now purchase Bitcoins from ATM's speaks volumes. The blockchain technology that supports Bitcoin is now considered to be the future of online financial transactions and supply chain management.

So now it is over to you. You need to take action and follow the advice in this guide. Reading this guide will make you smarter – taking action has the potential to make you richer. Remember to start small and use a reputable cryptocurrency exchange like Coinbase.com. Also get a secure wallet to transfer your Bitcoins and keep them safe.

If you see a cryptocurrency offer that looks too good to be true then it probably is. Avoid anything that claims to sell Bitcoins at way below market value or will guarantee returns. This is all a scam. Nobody can double your Bitcoins either so steer clear of this as well.

We hope that you found **Bitcoins and Tulipmania** informative and helpful. Get started today with your Bitcoin investing. We wish you every success on your cryptocurrency journey, and remember that you always need to keep learning. The smartest investors are the ones that usually make the highest profits!

www.ingramcontent.com/pod-product-compliance
Lightning Source LLC
Chambersburg PA
CBHW060521120726
48002CB00011B/3262